APR – 3 2012

SandCastle™
Animal Homes

Home
Sweet
Web

Mary Elizabeth Salzmann

CONSULTING EDITOR, DIANE CRAIG, M.A./READING SPECIALIST

A Division of ABDO
ABDO
Publishing Company

visit us at www.abdopublishing.com

Published by ABDO Publishing Company, a division of ABDO, P.O. Box 398166, Minneapolis, Minnesota 55439. Copyright © 2012 by Abdo Consulting Group, Inc. International copyrights reserved in all countries. No part of this book may be reproduced in any form without written permission from the publisher. SandCastle™ is a trademark and logo of ABDO Publishing Company.

Printed in the United States of America, North Mankato, Minnesota
062011
092011

 PRINTED ON RECYCLED PAPER

Editor: Katherine Hengel
Content Developer: Nancy Tuminelly
Cover and Interior Design and Production: Anders Hanson, Mighty Media, Inc.
Photo Credits: Shutterstock, iStockPhoto (Michael Pettigrew, Kris Hollingsworth)

Library of Congress Cataloging-in-Publication Data
Salzmann, Mary Elizabeth, 1968-
  Home sweet web / Mary Elizabeth Salzmann.
     p. cm. -- (Animal homes)
  ISBN 978-1-61714-820-0
  1. Embioptera--Juvenile literature. 2. Spider webs--Juvenile literature. 3. Animals--Habitations--Juvenile literature. I. Title.
  QL539.S25 2012
  591.56´4--dc22
                    2010053271

SANDCASTLE™ LEVEL: TRANSITIONAL

SandCastle™ books are created by a team of professional educators, reading specialists, and content developers around five essential components—phonemic awareness, phonics, vocabulary, text comprehension, and fluency—to assist young readers as they develop reading skills and strategies and increase their general knowledge. All books are written, reviewed, and leveled for guided reading, early reading intervention, and Accelerated Reader® programs for use in shared, guided, and independent reading and writing activities to support a balanced approach to literacy instruction. The SandCastle™ series has four levels that correspond to early literacy development. The levels are provided to help teachers and parents select appropriate books for young readers.

Emerging Readers
(no flags)

Beginning Readers
(1 flag)

Transitional Readers
(2 flags)

Fluent Readers
(3 flags)

Contents

What Is a Web? 4

Animals and Webs 6

Garden Spider 8

Black Widow Spider 10

Grass Spider 12

Wasp Spider 14

Funnel-web Wolf Spider 16

Tent Caterpillar 18

Webworm 20

Could You Live in a Web? 22

Quiz 23

Glossary 24

What Is a Web?

A web is a group of threads. Webs are made by spiders and some **insect larvae**. Spider and insect threads are called silk.

5

Animals and Webs

Most spiders live on their webs. They use webs to trap **prey**. Some **insect larvae** also make webs. They use the webs for shelter.

Garden spiders live on webs.

Garden spiders make orb webs. The spider waits in the middle of the web. The web traps the **prey**. Then the spider wraps the prey in silk.

9

Black widow spiders live on webs.

They make tangle webs to trap **prey**. They **inject poison** into their prey by biting them.

Grass spiders live on webs.

Grass spiders make funnel webs. The spider waits for the **prey** to land on the web. Then it runs out of the funnel and **grabs** the prey.

Wasp spiders live on webs.

Wasp spiders make webs in tall grass. It takes a wasp spider about an hour to finish a web.

Funnel-web wolf spiders live on webs.

Most wolf spiders do not make webs. The funnel-web wolf spider is different. It makes a funnel web that it uses for hunting and protection.

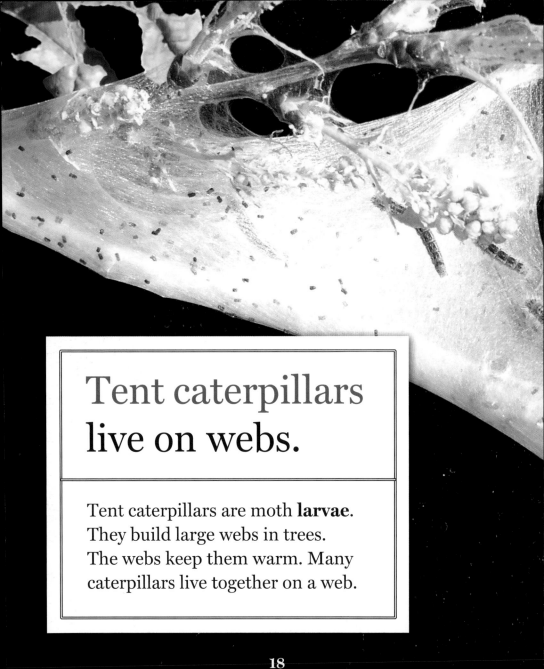

Tent caterpillars live on webs.

Tent caterpillars are moth **larvae**.
They build large webs in trees.
The webs keep them warm. Many
caterpillars live together on a web.

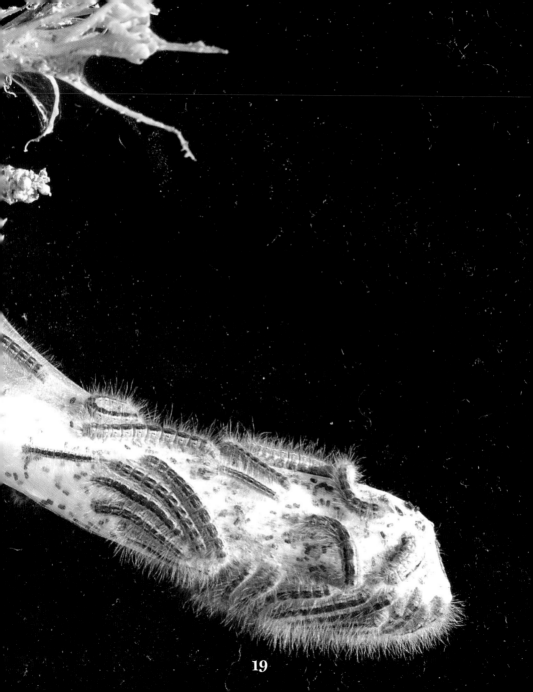

19

20

Webworms live in webs.

Fall webworms are moth **larvae**. Many of them live together in large webs. They eat leaves inside the web for about six weeks. Then they leave the web and get ready to become moths.

Could *you* live
on a web?

Quiz

1. Spiders are the only animals that make webs. *True or false?*

2. Garden spiders make orb webs. *True or false?*

3. Black widows do not bite their **prey**. *True or false?*

4. There are no wolf spiders that make webs. *True or false?*

5. Tent caterpillars live alone on their webs. *True or false?*

Glossary

grab – to take hold of something suddenly.

inject – to use something sharp, such as a needle or a stinger, to force a liquid into something.

insect – a small creature with two or four wings, six legs, and a body with three sections.

larva – a newly hatched wingless insect, before it transforms. *Larvae* is the plural of larva.

poison – a substance that can injure or kill.

prey – an animal that is hunted or caught for food.